Stories of Other Worlds

H. G. Wells

T0345618

Level 2

Retold by Annette Keen

Series Editors: Andy Hopkins and Jocelyn Potter

Pearson Education Limited

Edinburgh Gate, Harlow,
Essex CM20 2JE, England
and Associated Companies throughout the world.

ISBN: 978-1-4479-6749-1

This edition first published by Pearson Education Ltd 2010

5 7 9 10 8 6

Original text: Copyright by The Literary Executors of the Estate of H G Wells
This edition copyright © Pearson Education Ltd 2010

Illustrations by Adam Hunter Peck, Mike Lacey, Jamel Akhib,
Oxford Designers & Illustrators

The moral rights of the authors have been asserted in accordance with
the Copyright Designs and Patents Act 1988

Set in 12/15.5pt A. Garamond
Printed in China
SWTC/05

Published by Pearson Education Ltd

Acknowledgements
We are grateful to the following for permission to reproduce photographs:

(Key: b-bottom; c-centre; l-left; r-right; t-top)

Bridgeman Art Library Ltd: Yale University Art Gallery, New Haven, CT, USA 59l;
Corbis: Hulton-Deutsch Collection 59r

All other images © Pearson Education

For a complete list of the titles available in the Pearson English Active Readers series, visit www.pearsonenglishactivereaders.com.
Alternatively, write to your local Pearson Education office or to
Pearson English Readers Marketing Department, Pearson Education, Edinburgh Gate, Harlow, Essex CM20 2JE, England.

Contents

1.1 What's the book about?

1 Discuss these questions.

    a Think about the name of this book. What 'other worlds' can you think of?

    b H.G. Wells was a very famous writer. Do you know any of his work? Find out about him. What are many of his stories about?

2 Look at these pictures of people from each story. Which words describe them best? Write the words under the pictures.

....

....

interested   walking   excited   listening   laughing   unhappy

1.2 What happens first?

Read the name of the first story on page 1, and look at the picture. Then write the best words in these sentences.

1 The people in the village are ....
   (old / blind / stupid)

2 Their clothes are ....
   (expensive / dirty / strange)

3 The village looks ....
   (dangerous / clean / beautiful)

4 The story begins ....
   (in the future / now / in the past)

The Country of the Blind

'Look!' said one of the men. 'Look at his path through the snow!
He walked here. And he fell there.'

Our story begins in the Andes mountains of Ecuador, hundreds of years past. Between two great mountains there was a small, beautiful **valley**. It was a difficult, dangerous journey from the nearest town. One day, some people from Peru found the valley and they stayed there. The water was clean and there was fruit on the trees. Their animals gave them milk. There was no rain or snow, but the rivers from the mountains made the valley green. They could grow vegetables there. It was a wonderful place.

The people built a village in the valley, and their lives were happy. But then some of them were ill, and after this they couldn't see. New babies were born **blind** too. After many, many years, everybody in the valley was blind.

valley /ˈvæli/ (n) A *valley* is the flat ground between mountains. A river usually runs through it.
blind /blaɪnd/ (adj/n) *Blind* people (*the blind*) cannot see.

But in the time before that happened, some of the men had an answer to the problem.

'God is angry with us because there isn't a church in the village,' they said.

One man had a plan. 'Let's build a church,' he said. 'I'll go away, to the town, and buy the best things for our church. And I'll bring them back to our valley.'

The people gave him money. They did this happily because they didn't use money in the village.

'A new church will make God happy and then He will help us. We'll have our **sight** again,' they said.

So the young man made the difficult, dangerous journey over the mountains to the town. He told people in the town about his village and he visited many churches. Then he bought the things for the new church and he was ready for the journey home.

But one day when he was in the town, something very bad happened near his valley.

sight /saɪt/ (n) People without *sight* cannot see anything.

It was the middle of the day, but the sky suddenly went dark. The birds stopped singing. Animals put their heads up and listened. Then they started running away. There was a loud noise and the ground moved. The mountains moved and large **rocks** fell down into the valley. The people were very afraid. After some minutes it was quiet and everything stopped moving. Then the sun shone again and the birds sang.

But things were different. The country didn't look the same as before. The young man wanted to go back to his valley, but he couldn't find the way through the mountains. There were rocks across the mountain **paths** and there was no way past them. He couldn't get home to his wife and children in the valley. He had to stay in the town.

He told many people about his village, so more and more people heard the story of the Country of the Blind.

Hundreds of years later, another young man came into the story. His name was Nunez and he was a mountain climber from the Colombian city of Bogotá. He took some Englishmen on a journey, high in the Andes mountains.

rock /rɒk/ (n) You find large and small *rocks* on the ground. They often break off mountains.
path /pɑːθ/ (n) After a lot of people walk the same way for some time, their feet make a *path*.

They stopped for the night near the top of a mountain. Suddenly, they couldn't see Nunez.

'Nunez! Nunez, where are you?' they shouted.

They called to him, but he didn't answer. They couldn't sleep. In the morning they looked everywhere, but they couldn't find Nunez.

'Look!' said one of the men, 'Look at his path through the snow! He walked here. And he fell there.'

They looked down. A long, long way below, they could see the top of some trees. The trees were in a small valley at the bottom of the mountains. It was the Country of the Blind, but of course the Englishmen didn't know that.

'We have to get down there and find Nunez,' said one of them.

'Why? He's dead,' said another man.

'And we can't get there – there's no way down the mountain from here,' said a third man, 'only a very long fall.'

'We can do nothing. We can't help Nunez now. Let's go back.'

So the Englishmen left the mountain and went down to the town with their story of Nunez's fall.

But Nunez was not dead.

He fell through the snow, and then over the snow. He fell a thousand metres and more. The snow fell with him. It made a thick bed for him when he stopped falling. He didn't move for a long time. He was hurt, but he didn't die.

He looked up at the mountain, and he looked down into the valley. It was night, so he couldn't see the village.

'Perhaps I can get help in the morning,' he thought.

He moved slowly out of the snow. Then he found a warm place for the night and he went to sleep.

He woke up early the next morning, when the birds started to sing. Nunez sat up and looked round. He was near the valley at the bottom of the mountains. He could see some houses and a river below him.

'Somebody there will help me,' he thought.

He started walking down to the village. It was difficult because he was very tired. He went carefully because he didn't want to fall again.

By the end of the day he was at the river, and he stopped for a drink. There were beautiful flowers near the river.

'This is a lovely place,' Nunez thought.

There were a lot of small houses in the centre of the village. They looked very strange to him, because they didn't have any windows.

He could see men and women at work in the village. Some were in the **fields** with their children. He could see gardens near the houses and there were fine vegetables in them.

When Nunez was near the village, he shouted to some men.

'Hello!' he shouted. 'Hello ... hello!' and he **waved** his arms.

The men heard him and they turned their heads. They looked one way, and then the other way. They looked past Nunez, but they didn't look at him.

field /fiːld/ (n) A *field* is a big, open place in the country, for vegetables and other food.
wave /weɪv/ (v) When you *wave* at people, you move your arm above your head. Then they can see you.

'Why can't they see me?' he thought.

Nunez moved nearer and shouted again. He was now quite near three men. He waved again, but they didn't wave back to him.

'What's wrong with them?' he thought. 'Are they blind?'

He walked down to the men, and then he saw their faces. He was right – the men were all blind. They had no eyes.

'Who is this?' one man asked his friend. 'A man? Or is it a **spirit**?'

'It's a man,' said the second man. 'I think it's a man.'

Suddenly, Nunez understood. He remembered stories about this valley and he felt excited. It was a long and dangerous fall from the mountain, but here he was – in the Country of the Blind!

'He comes from the rocks,' said the third man. 'He walked out of the rocks and came to our village.'

The three men moved, all at the same time. They stood in front of Nunez and put their hands on his face. They felt his ears, his nose and his hair. One of them put his finger in Nunez's eye.

'What is this?' one of them asked. To these men, Nunez's eye was a strange thing. They didn't understand it.

'Be careful!' said Nunez.

spirit /ˈspɪrɪt/ (n) Some people think that they can see the *spirits* of dead people.

'He speaks,' said one of the men. 'So he's not an animal. But he's from the rocks.'

'And now he's in the world.' said another man.

'I *was* in the world,' said Nunez. 'I came out of the world. I came from the world over the mountains – from Bogotá, a very big city with thousands of people. People there can see. *I* can see.'

But the villagers didn't understand him.

'See?' said one of the men. 'What does he mean, Pedro? What is "see"? And there is no other world.'

'I remember stories about new men. They came out of the ground, like flowers. Perhaps this is a man like that,' said Pedro.

'A new man, only two or three days old,' said the other man.

'Take him into the village,' said Pedro. 'But shout first, Correa, or the children will be afraid.'

So Correa shouted, and the other two men put their hands on Nunez's arms. They **held** on to him. Then they started walking with Nunez between them.

hold /həʊld/ (v, past held) When something is in your hand, you *are holding* it. You *hold on* to something because you want it to stay with you.

'I can see the path,' said Nunez. 'You can take your hands away.'

But the men didn't take their hands away. Nunez could see the path, but they didn't know that. He could walk without their help. The men didn't understand this.

Some of the women and children arrived. They wanted to meet the strange man. They all wanted to feel his face with their fingers.

'He's a new man – he came from out of the rocks,' Pedro said to them. 'He's learning language. He uses strange words.'

Then Pedro held Nunez's hand and took him into the centre of the village.

'He's a man from the rocks,' Correa told people. 'His name is Bogotá.'

'No, I'm not from the rocks,' said Nunez. 'I come from the city of Bogotá. My city is over the mountains.'

Nobody in the village understood the word 'city'.

'Bogotá! Bogotá! His name is Bogotá!' the children said.

Nunez remembered his father's words: 'In the Country of the Blind, the man with one eye is **king**.'

'I'll be their king,' he thought. 'I can teach these people because I can see the world. I know more than they do. They'll want me to be their king.'

king /kɪŋ/ (n) The most important man in some countries is the *king*. Usually, his father was also the king.

9

2.1 Were you right?

Look back at your answers to Activity 1.2 on page iv. Then answer these questions.

1 Where is the village?

....

2 How many people there are blind when Nunez arrives?

....

3 Why don't other people go to the village?

....

2.2 What more did you learn?

1 **Write about this person.**

a What is his name?

....

b What is his job?

....

c Where does he come from?

....

2 **Put these sentences in the right order. Write the numbers 1–8.**

a ( ) Nunez waves to some men.

b ( ) The villagers think that Nunez is a new man.

c ( ) Nunez falls from the mountain.

d (1) The people want a church in the village.

e ( ) The Englishmen go back to the town.

f ( ) Nunez takes some climbers into the mountains.

g ( ) Nunez sees the village in the valley.

h ( ) The village men put their hands on Nunez's face.

2.3 Language in use

Read the sentences on the right. Then write sentences with could or *couldn't.*

> They **could** grow vegetables there.
>
> He **couldn't** get home to his wife and children.

1 Nunez / climb / mountains

....

2 The Englishmen / find / Nunez

....

3 Nunez / see / houses and a river

....

4 The village men / hear / Nunez

....

5 The men / see / Nunez

....

6 They / understand / all of Nunez's words

....

2.4 What's next?

1 Are these sentences right or wrong? What do you think? Talk about them with other students.

    a The villagers like Nunez more.
    b They are sad because they can't see.
    c They make Nunez their king.
    d They think that Nunez is very clever.
    e He marries a girl from the village.
    f He loses his sight.

2 Now look at the pictures in the second half of the story. What do they tell you? Do you want to change any of your answers to 1 a–f, above?

The Country of the Blind

'The problem with Bogotá is his eyes. They give him stupid ideas.
They move all the time and they stop him thinking.'

The men stopped at a house in the middle of the village. They wanted to show Nunez to the old men. The old men knew everything. They could tell the villagers about this strange new man.

The blind men pushed Nunez inside. It was very dark because there were no windows. Nunez couldn't see anything and he fell over somebody's feet. His arm hit somebody.

'Hold him down! Be careful! He wants to fight us,' said one of the men.

'I don't want to fight anybody,' said Nunez. 'I fell. I couldn't see, because it's very dark in here.'

But they didn't understand him.

'He uses words without meaning,' they said. 'It's because he's a new man. Perhaps he's also dangerous. We'll have to be careful.'

One of the old men started to question Nunez. Nunez wanted to tell them about the world outside their valley. But to the old men, their valley was the world. They didn't know anything about other places over the mountains.

They started to teach Nunez about their world.

'There was nothing here,' they told him. 'Only rock. First animals were born, and then men. And time is in two halves – warm time and cold time. People sleep in the warm time and work in the cold time.'

Nunez slowly understood. To blind men, warm and cold time were day and night. They couldn't see light and dark.

'That is different from my world,' he said.

The old men were quiet for a short time.

'Your world?' asked one of the men. 'What do you mean? Your world was the rocks. There's nothing different there.'

'Don't think of the past,' said another man. 'We can teach you everything. One day you'll be as clever as we are.'

Nunez was very hungry. He asked for some food, and they gave him bread and milk. Then they left him, but he couldn't sleep.

Four days came and went. Nunez started to work in the fields with the blind people. But he was from the city. He knew nothing about this work.

'You don't know much,' they told him, 'but we can teach you. You'll learn many things from us.'

'When I'm king, I'll make changes,' Nunez thought. 'First, I'll change the hours of work. I don't like working at night and sleeping in the day.'

But the blind people didn't want him to be their king, and he couldn't understand why.

He started to learn more about the blind people. They worked hard, but only because they had to have food and clothes. They enjoyed singing and making music. There was love between them, and their children were happy. They could hear very well – better than Nunez.

Sometimes, he told the people about the beautiful world outside the village.

'The sky is often very blue. There are flowers of every colour, and birds fly high above us. The mountains are wonderful. You can't see the tops of them.'

But they laughed at him. To them he was a stupid man with strange ideas.

'You talk about your home over the mountains,' said one of them, 'but there's nothing past the rocks. That's the end of the world.'

Sometimes, a lovely young woman sat with them. She never spoke, but she listened to Nunez. He was happy when she was there. Her name was Medina-saroté.

The blind people often called Nunez 'stupid', and one day he was tired of it.

It was a work day (but night to Nunez), and he was in the fields. He took his **spade** in his hands. Suddenly, he felt very angry and he wanted to hit somebody with it. He stood and held his spade. He looked at the blind people near him.

He could easily hit one of them. But something stopped him.

The blind people heard. They knew. They all stopped work and turned to him.

'Put down that spade,' one of them said.

'You don't understand me,' he said. 'You're blind, and I can see.' But he knew now – he couldn't hit a blind man. And he couldn't fight men with very different ideas.

Nunez pushed one of the men very hard. The man fell and Nunez ran past him, across the village. He ran through the streets. He looked

spade /speɪd/ (n) You use a *spade* when you work in the garden. You use one before you put a new tree in the ground.

behind him and saw the blind men.

'They're coming after me,' he thought. 'They can't see me, but they know. They know that I'm running.'

'Bogotá!' they called. 'Bogotá, where are you?'

He held his spade. He heard the words in his head: 'In the Country of the Blind, the man with one eye is king!' But he couldn't get away from the men. He watched them and waited.

'They know I'm here,' he thought. 'And they want to catch me.'

He called to them, 'You're always telling me that I'm stupid. But you're wrong, I'm an intelligent man. And I want to do different things with my life.'

The men walked quickly, with their arms in front of them. Suddenly, they were all round him.

'Bogotá! Put down that spade,' they said again.

'I'll hit you!' he said. 'Go away or I'll hurt somebody.'

Nunez started to run again. He ran past two of the men. He hit one of them on the arm with his spade. The man went down. He ran past them!

He ran past a street of houses. He could hear the blind men's feet behind him. He found the bridge and he ran across it. He went past animals in the fields. He jumped over the village wall and climbed up into the rocks. Then he fell to the ground and started to cry.

He stayed outside the village wall for two nights and two days. He could never be king in this place. He understood that now. He could not fight the blind people. He was hungry, thirsty and cold. Without them, he was dead.

On the third day he went down to the wall and cried for help.

Two blind men came to the wall and talked to him.

'I was stupid,' he said. 'But I'm only a new man from the rocks. I know nothing. Please help me.'

'That's better,' they said. 'And can you "see" now?'

'No,' he said. 'That was stupid. The word doesn't mean anything.' He cried again. 'Please give me some food or I'll die.'

He was ill for some days, but the blind people looked after him. They came and talked to him. They were kind.

So Nunez lived in the Country of the Blind, and he was not unhappy. He worked for Pedro's uncle, Yacob, and Yacob was kind to Nunez. Yacob's daughter was Medina-saroté.

'She's very beautiful,' Nunez thought. He started to work or sit near her as often as possible. One day they listened to the village music and he took her hand. The next evening, they ate their dinner at the same table and Medina-saroté put her hand in his.

The day after that, they walked away from the other people. Nunez wanted to speak to her.

'I love you,' he said. 'I think you love me too.'

Medina-saroté smiled her lovely smile at him.

'Yes, Nunez. I think I do.'

After that, they talked very often. He spoke of the beautiful things in the world outside the valley. It wasn't his world now, but he wanted to tell her. She didn't understand his stories, but she liked to hear them.

But there was a problem. Her sisters didn't like Nunez and they told Yacob about him and Medina-saroté.

'We're in love,' said Nunez. 'We want to marry.'

Medina-saroté's father and sisters weren't happy about this.

'Nunez is nice, but stupid,' they thought. They didn't want him in their family.

Medina-saroté cried when her father told her. She was very sad.

'But my dear daughter, he's a strange man, different from us. And he has very stupid ideas,' said Yacob.

'I know,' she cried. 'But he's better than he was. And he's strong, dear Father, and kind. He loves me – and, Father, I love him.'

Yacob was sorry because his youngest daughter was very unhappy. Also, he liked Nunez in many ways. So he went to the old men of the village.

'He's better than he was,' said Yacob. 'Perhaps one day he'll be as clever as we are. And I think he's a good man.'

One of the old men had an idea.

'I think I understand the problem with Bogotá,' he said. 'It's his "eyes". They give him stupid ideas. They move all the time and they stop him thinking.'

'What can we do?' asked Yacob.

'It's easy. We can take out his eyes.'

'And then he'll be all right?'

'Yes. Then he'll be one of us.'

Yacob was very happy. He went quickly to Nunez.

'There's an answer to your problem,' he said. 'Without your eyes, you can marry Medina-saroté.'

Nunez wasn't happy with this idea, and he told Medina-saroté.

'I won't see anything then. Do you want me to lose my sight? I won't see the beautiful flowers, or the sky. And I won't see you, my love. Do you really want that?'

'I love to hear your pretty talk … but …'

Nunez knew then. Medina-saroté loved him, but she didn't understand. He felt angry, but also sorry for her. He put his arm round her, and they sat for some time.

'I don't want to lose you,' he said, 'so I'll do this.'

On the last day before they took out his eyes, Nunez saw Medina-saroté for a short time.

'After tomorrow,' he said, 'I shall see nothing.'

'The old men won't hurt you much,' she said. 'You're doing this for me, and I love you for that.'

They said goodbye. Nunez looked at her lovely face again. He wanted to remember it every day. Then he walked away.

He walked past the houses, and through the wall round the village. He sat on the rocks and looked back at the valley. Then he looked up at the mountains. They were beautiful. The sky was blue and the snow shone in the sun. Nunez thought of the world behind the mountains – his world. He thought of rivers and the sea. He thought of his family and friends. And he thought of Bogotá.

Nunez looked again at the village and remembered Medina-saroté.

'I love her very much,' he thought. 'She wants us to marry, but it's very difficult. I don't think I can. I don't want her to be unhappy, but I can't stay there. I can't live without my sight.'

He looked down at the village and he felt very sad.

'The Country of the Blind will never be my home. Medina-saroté and I will never be happy. I was wrong.'

Then he turned to the mountains, and he started to climb.

When the sun went down, Nunez was a long way from the Country of the Blind, and very high. He saw a little orange flower on a rock. He looked at it and smiled.

Night came. Nunez wanted to sleep, but he couldn't. He looked up at the cold sky and he smiled. In a strange way, he was happy again.

3.1 Were you right?

Remember your answers to Activity 2.4. Then answer these questions.
Write (✓) or (✗).

1 Why does Nunez think he will be king?

a He is clever. ◯

b He is young. ◯

c He can see. ◯

d He has good ideas. ◯

e He is stronger than the villagers. ◯

f He works harder than them. ◯

2 What do the villagers think of him?

a He is clever. ◯

b He is young. ◯

c He can see. ◯

d He is nice. ◯

e He doesn't know much. ◯

f He knows more than them. ◯

3.2 What more did you learn?

Finish the sentences with the
words on the right.

1 Nunez wants to marry   but she doesn't understand him.

2 He wants to tell Medina-saroté   nice, but stupid.

3 Her sisters think that Nunez is   Yacob's youngest daughter.

4 Yacob is sorry for his daughter   because he can't live without his sight.

5 Nunez can marry Medina-saroté   because she is very unhappy.

6 Medina-saroté loves Nunez   but he has to be blind.

7 Nunez can't marry her   about the beautiful things in the world.

3.3 Language in use

Read the sentences on the right. Then answer the questions below.

> It was very dark **because** there were no windows.
>
> 'I don't want to lose you, **so** I'll do this.'

1 He knew nothing about this work. He was from the city.

   He knew nothing about this work because he was from the city.

2 'I'll change the hours of work. I don't like working at night.'

   ....

   ....

3 'There's nothing past the rocks. That's the end of the world.'

   ....

   ....

4 'I'm only a new man from the rocks. I know nothing.'

   ....

   ....

5 'His "eyes" move all the time. They stop him thinking.'

   ....

   ....

6 'I can't stay there. I can't live without my sight.'

   ....

   ....

3.4 What's next?

The next story is 'The Door in the Wall'. Look at the sentence in *italics* and the picture on the next page. Discuss these questions.

1 What do you think is behind the door?

2 Do you think these two men are brothers? Why (not)?

3 Where do you think they are?

4 What are they doing?

5 What time is this story about: the past, the future, or now?

The Door in the Wall

'There was a London street outside the door, but inside was a different world.
When the door closed behind me, I forgot about London, and home.'

My friend Lionel Wallace told me about the Door in the Wall. We were old friends from school. When we first met, we were only children. After we left school, we did not meet very often. But that evening we were in a restaurant in London. We ate dinner and Wallace told me his story. At the time I **believed** it.

Wallace's story made the evening more interesting. I thought about it more after I went home. Was it perhaps *only* a story? By the next morning, there was no question about it. I did not believe the story.

But Wallace died a short time after that evening. He died in a strange way. Then I knew. To Wallace, it was not only a story. He believed in the Door in the Wall.

The food that night was good and we asked for a second bottle of wine. We talked about a strange story in the newspaper. I think I said something about **ghosts**. Then he started to tell his story.

'I don't know about ghosts, Redmond,' he said. 'But there is something like that in my life. It isn't a spirit or a ghost, but a place.'

---

believe /bɪˈliːv/ (v) When, to you, something is right, you *believe* it. You can also believe in an idea or a person.
ghost /ɡəʊst/ (n) Some people think that *ghosts* are the spirits of dead people.

He looked sad. It was difficult for him, but he wanted to tell me his story. At the time, Wallace was nearly forty years old. He was a very clever and important man. He could do many things. But Wallace did not usually tell stories. Some men can tell interesting stories well, but not Wallace. So I listened carefully to this story.

'I remember when I saw the Door in the Wall for the first time,' he said. 'I was a little boy of about five years old.'

Wallace was a clever child, from a rich family. They lived in a big, expensive house in west London. His mother was dead and his father was a very busy man. He did not play with his son. He worked all the time. A woman came to the house every day and she looked after the little boy.

'I was often bored at home. One day I walked out of our garden and down the road. I don't remember the streets. But I remember the white wall and the green door. It was a sunny, autumn day – October, I think. The trees near the door were red and brown.'

Wallace spoke very quietly.

'I wanted to go through the door. But my father wouldn't like it. I knew this. He was often angry with me. So I walked past the door to the end of the road. I waited there for a minute and thought about it. Then

I turned round and ran back to the door. Before I could think again, I pushed it open. And then I walked through it.'

So Wallace walked into another world. He walked into the beautiful garden behind the Door in the Wall. After that, he never forgot it. He thought about it every day of his life.

'Everything was beautiful there,' he said. 'There were two big **panthers**, but I wasn't afraid of them. I put my hands on their heads and they walked with me. We walked through the garden. It was a very big garden and I couldn't see to the end. There was a London street outside the door, but inside was a different world. When the door closed behind me, I forgot about London, and home.

'There was a long, wide path with flowers on the right and on the left of it. They were the most wonderful flowers, of every colour. I felt very

panther /ˈpænθə/ (n) A *panther* is a large, black animal – a big cat.

happy in that lovely place, with the two panthers next to me. A tall girl met me on the path. She smiled and took my hand. We walked down the path and up some wide, red stairs. Here there were dark trees. Beautiful white birds flew above us.

Wallace stopped for a minute.

'Yes?' I said.

'There were people in the garden. I remember them. They were all beautiful and kind. There was love in their eyes. And there were other children. This was important to me, because I didn't have many friends. These children played with me – but …'

Wallace stopped again. I understood why.

'What can't you remember?' I asked.

'You are right. I played games with the children, but I can never remember those games. I was happy with the other children. Then a woman came and took me up some stairs. The boys and girls called to me: "Come back to us!" The woman showed me a book and we turned the pages. It was a book about me. It was my story. I saw pictures of my mother and father, and my home. Then I saw the green door and the white wall. In the picture I stood outside with my hand on the door.

'I looked up at the woman. "Next?" I asked her. She put her hand on mine and smiled. I turned the page. But the next picture didn't show the garden. It was a picture of a busy, grey London street. And then I was really outside the garden again. I stood in the street and I cried. There was no green door, so I couldn't get back to my new friends. I was lost and afraid. An old man came past and stopped. He wanted to help me.

'"Are you lost, little boy?" he asked me.

'But I couldn't answer him. I cried and cried. Later, a young policeman took me home.

'My father was angry. I told him about the garden, but he didn't believe me. "Don't talk about this again," he said.'

'Did you look for the garden?' I asked.

'No,' he said. 'I think my father watched me more after that. He was very careful with me. I didn't look for the Door in the Wall, but I didn't forget it. And then I found it again suddenly, years later. It was near the school.'

'But our school wasn't in west London,' I said. 'And the garden was in a street near your home.'

'Yes, that was very strange. I wanted to find a different way to school. I walked down a street and turned left. I didn't know this street. And then I couldn't find the way. I was lost. It was nearly time for school and I didn't want to be late. I ran from one street to the next. Suddenly, there was the white wall, and the green door. I think I wanted to go inside. I was interested, but I didn't push the door. I looked at my watch. There were only ten minutes before school started. I ran to the next street and found the right way. I arrived at school in time.'

'And later that day? Did you want to go back after school?' I asked.

Wallace thought about this.

'Perhaps, but I didn't go back. Do you remember young Hopkins? He walked home with me that day. I wanted to tell somebody. So I told him about the garden. The next day he told a lot of other, bigger boys. They didn't believe it and they laughed at me. "I'll take you there," I said. "It's only ten minutes from here." I was a little afraid of those big boys.

'But we never found the white wall and the green door.'

'What do you mean?'

'I couldn't find it. Later, I went again without the other boys, but I couldn't find the right street. It wasn't there.'

'And the other boys … were they unkind?'

'Yes, they were very unkind to me. Every night I cried. My schoolwork was bad and I was very unhappy. I was usually the best in our class at English. But that year *you* came top, do you remember? After that, I started to work hard again. I never spoke of the garden again at school.'

4.1 Were you right?

Think about your answers to Activity 3.4. Then choose the right words for these sentences.

1 Wallace and Redmond *work in the same office / are old friends / are strangers.*

2 They are at *a hotel / Wallace's home / a restaurant.*

3 Wallace is *telling a story / listening to a story / talking about business.*

4 Behind the door was *a wall / a London street / a beautiful garden.*

5 Wallace's story started when he was *at university / at school / a little boy.*

4.2 What more did you learn?

Who said these words? Where were they? Use words from the boxes below.

1 'It's only ten minutes from here.'

....

....

2 'Come back to us!'

....

....

3 'Next?'

....

....

4 'Are you lost, little boy?'

....

....

5 'Don't talk about this again.'

....

....

WHO?	WHERE?
Wallace's father	in the garden
an old man	at school
Wallace	in the street
other children	in Wallace's home

4.3 Language in use

**Read the sentences on the right.
Then look at the pictures below
and finish the sentences.**

> **When** we first met, we were only children.
>
> **When** the door closed behind me, I forgot about London, and home.

1 When Wallace started his story,
  Redmond listened carefully .

2 It was a sunny, autumn day when

....

3 Wallace wasn't afraid when

....

4 When a policeman took Wallace home,

....

5 When he told other children about the door,

....

.4 What's next?

**Look at the pictures in Part 2 of the story. What do you think will
happen? Write Yes or No next to the sentences.**

1 Wallace will never find the garden again. ....

2 He will see the garden many more times. ....

3 He will open the door, but the garden will be different. ....

4 He will open the door, but the garden won't be there. ....

5 He will go into the garden and the panthers will kill him. ....

The Door in the Wall

'I walk with nobody, and I have only one idea in my head.
I think of a door, a wall and a garden.'

For a short time, my friend looked into the fire without speaking. Then he said, 'I didn't see it again for years. But I did see it.'

'Do you mean the garden?'

'Not the garden – the Door in the Wall. I was seventeen,' he said. 'I was on my way to Oxford, for my first day at university. We drove through London and I looked out of the window. Suddenly, there was the wall – and the door. I wanted to stop the taxi. I asked the driver … but then I looked at my watch. No, I thought, we don't have much time. So we didn't stop because I didn't want to be late.

'I started to see a different open door – the door to my **career**.'
Wallace looked again into the fire. The red light shone on his face.

'I followed my career and I worked hard. Now, I am nearly at the top of my career. But through the years I thought of the garden a thousand times.'

'Did you see the door again?' I asked.

'Three times,' he said. 'But I was always too busy, and I didn't go in. And my world was interesting. I didn't want to be with the panthers and the tall girl. I was interested in other things. There were dinners in the best hotels with pretty women. And my career was very important to me.

'One afternoon – the first time – I walked down a road in London. It was somewhere new to me, a different place. I turned left into a small street, and there were the white wall and the green door. But I had to see somebody important that day. I had to be at his office. There was no time for the garden on that day.'

career /kə'rɪə/ (n) Your *career* is your work. After you study for this work, you do better and better jobs.

Wallace thought about the garden for years, but then he did not go in!

'Were you sorry?' I asked.

'Not at the time, but later – yes, I was very sorry. And sad too. Years of hard work followed that day. I didn't see the door in all that time.'

Wallace looked across the table at me. He spoke very sadly.

'But now something is different. Now the garden calls to me more often than before. I don't understand why. On two different days this year I saw the door and I had to walk past. Each time I stayed outside and I didn't go into the garden. Each time there was something more important in my life. The first time was the night when my father died. I wanted to see him before he died. I didn't have much time, so I walked past the door.

'The second time, I was with two other men. They were important people and they could help me with my career.

'I saw the door. I wanted to stop, but I couldn't. It was the wrong time for me. I couldn't walk into the garden that day. "They will think I am very stupid," I thought. "I have to walk past." So I did.

'But I tell you this, Redmond. Next time I see the door, I will go through into the garden. I will go and never come back.'

'I believe you will,' I said. 'But how will you find it again? Where will you look for it?'

'I don't know,' he said. 'Sometimes I feel it is lost to me now. I didn't go through it, and now I cannot. I think my time for the garden was in the past, not the future.'

My friend looked very sad. I wanted to help him, but what could I do?

'Perhaps you are wrong. How do you know this?' I asked.

'I know, I know. I don't think I will see it again.'

'Don't believe that! Wait, and it will come again!' I said.

'I will tell you something, Redmond,' said Wallace. 'At nights, I go out and walk the streets. In the dark, people don't know me. Me! An important man, a man with a wonderful career! I walk and walk. I have only one idea in my head. I think of a door, a wall and a garden.'

Sometimes, I think of that night in the restaurant. I think of Wallace's white face. He was very unhappy. I remember his strange story. I hear his words again.

I remember him very well tonight.

Yesterday's London newspaper is on my chair. It is open at the second page. The story about Wallace is on that page.

He is dead.

Everybody talked about it today. At lunch there was no other conversation. We all spoke about him, but I said nothing about Wallace's garden.

He died in a very strange way. They found him a long way down a big **hole** at East Kensington Station.

They are building a new station for the underground trains. You cannot see the hole from the street, because there is a wall round it. They built this so people couldn't fall in the hole.

But Wallace fell in, because there was a small door cut into the wall.

The builders used the door in the wall. Somebody closed it each night, but last night they forgot. Wallace pushed it open and fell into the hole behind the door.

The newspaper told the story. Wallace left his office and started to walk home. This was not strange – he often walked home at night. In my head I can see a picture of him. He is walking, in the dark. He is near

hole /həʊl/ (n) You make a *hole* in the ground with a spade.

the station. The lights there are not very good. I can see him in the quiet street, late at night. He is the only person there.

Did the wall look white under those lights? Did that small, open door look green? Did Wallace think, 'That is *my* wall, and that is *my* door.' I believe that he did.

'This time,' he thought, 'I will go in.' He pushed the door, and it opened. He walked through it. He told me, 'Next time I won't come back.' And he was right.

Perhaps there never was a door in a wall. Perhaps it was only an idea in his head. The garden was never really there. I don't know. But I know he wanted that garden.

I told you his story in his words. But now I know the end of the story.

5.1 Were you right?

Look back at your answers to Activity 4.4. Then put the right words in the story below.

When Wallace saw the door again, he was [1]........................... years old. He couldn't stop, because he was on his way to [2]..........................., in Oxford. He thought [3]........................... the garden many times after this. He saw the door [4]........................... more times. He didn't go in because he was always too [5].......................... . Then one night, after he tells his story to Redmond, he is walking in a quiet street near a [6].......................... . He sees the [7].......................... again. He opens it, but there is no [8].......................... behind it. He falls into a [9].......................... and dies.

5.2 What more did you learn?

Look at the pictures. How are these important to the story? Write a sentence next to each one.

1 ....
....
....
....
....

2 ....
....
....
....
....

3 ....
....
....
....
....

5.3 Language in use

Read the sentences in the box. Then write sentences with *had to* and the verbs in *italics*.

> I **had to see** somebody important that day.
>
> I **had to be** at his office.

1 Wallace saw the door from the taxi. There wasn't time to stop. *(drive)*

 <u>He had to drive past the door.</u>

2 His father was very ill. Wallace couldn't go through the door. *(visit)*

 ....

3 He was with two men. They were important for his career. *(stay)*

 ....

4 His life was unhappy. He looked for the garden. *(find)*

 ....

5 Wallace saw the door again. He had a lot of time. *(go)*

 ....

5.4 What's next?

The next story is 'The Young Ghost'. Look at the words in *italics* at the top of the next page. Then look at the picture and discuss the people in it. Who are they? What are they talking about? Why? What do you think? Make notes below.

Notes

The Young Ghost

'We forget. People stay the same after they die. A good person will be a good ghost.
A stupid person will be a stupid ghost.'

I remember that day at the hotel. I remember Clayton's last story. I can see us all now, in the dining-room. Our good friends Sanderson, Evans and Wish were there. We four arrived at the hotel that Saturday morning and met Clayton there.

'I came last night,' he said. 'I wanted to be here early this morning.'

We played tennis and we walked in the country. Later, we went back to the hotel and enjoyed a very good dinner.

We felt warm and happy in the hotel dining-room. Clayton sat next to the large open fire and smoked his cigarette. He liked telling stories, and wanted to tell us one now. We did not always believe Clayton's stories, but they were usually interesting. Sometimes, they were very funny too.

'You know, ' he said, after a short time. 'I was the only person in the hotel last night.'

'Were there no waiters here?' asked Wish. 'Or waitresses?'

'Yes, of course *they* were here, but they sleep on the top floor of the hotel,' said Clayton. 'I was the only visitor.' Then he said, quite quietly, 'I caught a ghost!'

'Caught a ghost?' said Sanderson. 'Where is it?'

Evans was very excited. He stood up and shouted, 'You caught a ghost, Clayton? I'd like to hear more! Tell us about it!'

'I will, in a minute,' said Clayton, 'but first please close the door, Evans. We don't want anybody to hear us. This is a very old building and some people don't like the idea of ghosts near them.'

Evans shut the door and sat down again.

'He wasn't a very good ghost. I don't think he will come again,' said Clayton.

'And where is it?' asked Sanderson. He looked round the room. We all looked.

'He isn't here now. He went away,' said Clayton. 'He wanted to go, and I helped him.'

'I'm sorry about that,' said Sanderson. 'I never met a ghost in my life.'

We all laughed, but Clayton didn't laugh with us.

'I know you don't believe me,' he said. 'But this really was a ghost.'

Nobody spoke for a minute or two.

'It was very strange – the strangest thing in my life. Before that, I didn't believe in ghosts. But then there was one in my room.'

He lit another cigarette.

'Did you talk to him?' asked Wish.

'Oh, yes. For about an hour.'

'So he enjoyed a good conversation,' I said with a smile.

'He wanted to talk,' said Clayton. 'He had a problem.'

'Did he cry?' somebody asked.

'Yes, he cried some of the time,' said Clayton. He looked quite sad when he remembered his conversation with the ghost. 'Ghosts have a difficult time,' he said. 'I didn't know that. It isn't easy for them, you know.'

We all waited. Nobody wanted Clayton to tell his story quickly.

'We forget,' Clayton continued. 'People stay the same after they die. A good person will be a good ghost. A stupid person will be a stupid ghost. People don't change. This was the weak ghost of a very weak young man.'

Clayton looked into the fire.

'I first saw him outside my room. I could see through him. He was in front of the window, but I could see the window through his back.'

'Were you afraid?' I asked.

'No, I wasn't,' said Clayton. 'He couldn't hurt me – he was very weak. I could see that.'

'How did he look?' asked Wish.

'He had one hand on the wall, and the other hand in front of his mouth. He was young and thin, with big ears. His clothes weren't good –

they were cheap clothes.'

'So what happened next?' I asked.

'I came up the stairs very quietly. I stopped at the top and looked at him. I wasn't afraid, but I was interested in him.'

'How long were you there?' asked Evans.

'Not more than a minute. He turned and saw me. For a short time, I looked at him and he looked at me. Then he remembered. He was a ghost. He put his arms up above his head and said a quiet "*Boo-ooo.*"

'"*Boo!* Don't be stupid," I said. "Who are you? Why are you here?"'

Clayton drank a little more of his wine. Nobody spoke. We always enjoyed Clayton's stories and this was one of his best. We waited quietly and then he started to speak again.

'He looked a little sad. "*Boo-oo,*" he said again. I wasn't afraid of him. I wanted him to know that. So I walked through his arm.

'"Are you staying in this hotel?" I asked him.

'He moved away a little and looked down at the floor.

'"No, I'm not staying here," he said. "I'm a ghost."'

Evans asked a question. 'How did he sound, Clayton?'

Clayton thought for a minute.

'He sounded weak. He was the ghost of a weak young man. He sounded unhappy too.

'"Who do you want to see?" I asked him. "Me? Or one of the waiters, perhaps?" He didn't answer me, so I tried again. "What are you doing here?" I asked. He put his hands down and stopped making the "*boo-oo*" noise. We stood for a minute. I looked at him and he looked at the floor.

'"I'm **haunting**." he said.

'"You can't do that here," I said, quietly. "People won't like it."

'"But I'm a ghost," he said. "I have to haunt. All of us do."

'"This is a hotel," I said. "People often stay here with children. Think of the problems! Children are afraid of ghosts. Didn't you think of that?"

'"No, sir," he said sadly. "I didn't."'

haunt /hɔːnt/ (v) Ghosts *haunt* people or places when they visit them.

Sanderson laughed.

'Not a very intelligent ghost,' he said.

'You're right,' said Clayton. 'I wanted to know more about this unhappy ghost, so I asked him some questions.

'"Did you live here? Did you die here?" I asked him.

'"No, sir," he said. "I came here because it's a very old hotel. It's a good place for haunting."

'"No it isn't – you're wrong," I said. "Now go away! Go before the morning comes."

'He looked down at his feet. "What are you waiting for?" I asked.

'"There's a problem," he said. "I can't go back. I came here last night at midnight for some haunting. It was my first time. I went into the cupboards in some of the bedrooms and I waited. But nobody came. There was nobody here. I couldn't haunt anybody. I walked up and down the stairs, but I didn't see anybody there. Now I want to get back and I can't. I can't remember how."

'"This is very strange," I said to him. He looked at me very sadly and I couldn't be angry with him. Then I heard somebody downstairs. "I don't understand the problem. Come into my room and tell me more about it," I said to him.

'I wanted to hold his arm, but it wasn't possible. There was nothing in my hand. But we went to my room and I closed the door.'

'"Here we are," I said to him. I sat down on a chair next to the window. "Sit down and tell me all about it. I think you have quite a difficult problem."'

'And did he sit down?' asked Evans. 'Can ghosts sit?'

'This ghost didn't sit down. He wanted to move round the room. But we talked for quite a long time.

'It was really very strange. There I was in my nice, clean bedroom. And there was this ghost with me. He moved from the door to the window, then back again to the door. He moved all the time. And I could see through him. I could see the **candles** through him, and the pictures on the wall. It felt very strange.'

candle /ˈkændl/ (n) In the past, people used *candles* in their rooms for light.

6.1 Were you right?

Look back at your notes in Activity 5.4. Then answer the questions with names from the box.

> the writer   Sanderson
> Wish   Evans   Clayton
> all of them

1 Who arrives at the hotel on Friday evening? ....

2 Who plays tennis on Saturday? ....

3 Who closes the dining-room door? ....

4 Who says that he never met a ghost? ....

5 Who asks Clayton: 'Did you talk to him? ....

6 Who says, 'So he enjoyed a good conversation.' ....

6.2 What more did you learn?

Match the sentences to the pictures.

1 He was a weak young man.

2 He wanted to haunt the hotel.

3 He caught a ghost.

4 He couldn't leave.

5 He was not afraid.

6 He was not happy.

7 He had a big problem.

8 He wanted to help.

5.3 Language in use

Read the sentences in the box on the right. Then finish each sentence below with one of these words.

> **Nobody** spoke for a minute or two.
>
> 'We don't want **anybody** to hear us.'

> anybody nothing everybody something
> nobody anything everything

1 .... enjoyed Clayton's stories.

2 .... wanted the story to end too quickly.

3 Clayton saw .... at the top of the stairs.

4 The ghost didn't know .... about haunting.

5 The ghost didn't haunt .... before Clayton arrived.

6 .... was difficult for the weak young ghost.

7 When Clayton took the ghost's arm, there was .... in his hand.

.4 What's next?

Read the sentences in *italics* at the top of the next page. Do you think that is the end of the story? Here are some other possible endings. Which do you think is the best? Discuss them with other students and number them 1 (the best) to 6 (the worst).

a The ghost can't leave the hotel. He learns more about haunting and is a better ghost. ◯

b The ghost goes back to the ghost world and takes Clayton with him. ◯

c The ghost moves between the ghost world and our world. He often visits Clayton. ◯

d Other ghosts come to the hotel. They help the young ghost and he finds his way to the other world. ◯

e Clayton dies, and visits the young ghost in his world. ◯

f Clayton tells his friends, 'It was only a story.' ◯

The Young Ghost

'And then he went! He wasn't there! I turned back to the room,
but there was nobody there.'

'What did you talk about when the ghost was in your room?' asked Wish.

'Did he tell you about his life?' asked Sanderson.

We wanted to know more about our friend's visitor. We started to believe Clayton too. It was only a story when he started, and Clayton told very good stories. But now it was more than that. We believed it.

'And when did he die?' Evans asked.

'Only last month. He's a new ghost, and not very good at it. He doesn't understand much about haunting.'

'How did he die?'

'That,' said Clayton, 'is the most interesting thing about him. He worked as an English teacher in a London boys' school. He lived in a small room in the school. Some of the boys also lived there. One night, he heard a sound. "I never slept well," he said. "When I heard a small sound, my eyes always opened again." He took a candle and went downstairs, to the school office. There was an old **gas** fire in the room. The fire wasn't lit, and there was gas in the room. His candle lit the gas. There was a very loud noise … and then a fire started. He died in the fire.'

'That was a very bad end to his life,' Wish said.

'And the schoolboys? What happened to them?' I asked.

'They were all right. Somebody saw the fire and put it out. It didn't go up to the bedrooms. But it was too late for my ghost.'

Clayton lit another cigarette and looked into the fire in the hotel dining-room.

---

gas /gæs/ (n) Many people have *gas* fires in their homes. You can't see gas.

'Who was this ghost, when he lived?' I asked.

'I don't know his name – he didn't tell me. But he wasn't important. He didn't have a very interesting life,' said Clayton. 'He wasn't clever, rich or funny. He had a boring life and now he's a boring ghost. He really didn't enjoy his life.'

'He told you this?' asked Wish.

'That's right. When he moved across my bedroom, he was smoke in the wind. He talked and talked, and it was a thin sound. The sound of a thin, stupid, boring man.'

'Did he have a family? A wife? Children, perhaps? Or friends?' asked Wish.

'He talked about his mother and father and his schoolteacher. I don't think he had any good friends all his life. He had a girlfriend. He wanted to marry her. He talked about her, and she sounded quite boring too. But the fire ended everything for him,' Clayton said.

'I asked him, "And where are you now?" He didn't really know the answer to that. He talked about a place for new ghosts. It was a strange world, very different from ours. Ghosts stay there for some time.'

'So there were other ghosts with him?' I asked.

'Oh, yes,' said Clayton. 'A lot of other young men. They were all a little stupid, and they often talked about haunting. It was a game to them. Most of them didn't haunt – they only talked about it. But our friend heard them. He wanted to try haunting. "I remembered pictures of ghosts and haunting," he said. "It looked easy. I wasn't very good at most things. Perhaps I could be good at this. So I came here." He was wrong about that. He wasn't very good at haunting.'

'And how did he feel about that?' I asked.

'He was very unhappy. He wanted to be a good ghost, but he wasn't. When he told me all of this, he looked very sad. I think I was his first friend. "Nobody in my life was as kind to me as you are now," he said.

'I didn't want to be kind. I wanted him to leave my bedroom. I said, "Haunting isn't easy. You had some problems here. But don't think about that now. Go back now to the other world and forget about this haunting." "I can't get back there," he said unhappily. "I try, but I can't do it." "Try again," I said to him. So he did.'

'He tried?' said Sanderson. 'How?'

'With **gestures**,' said Clayton. 'Hand gestures. He got here that way. He had to get back the same way.'

'But how could he do that?' I asked.

Clayton walked across the room. We all followed him with our eyes.

'It's difficult,' he said. 'There were a lot of different gestures. I can't tell you everything, but perhaps I can show you. He moved his hands and waved his arms.' Clayton's arms flew round his head. 'He gestured this way, and that way. He did it again and again. But each time, he forgot something.

'It was very strange. We were there in my bedroom. It was very quiet. There was no sound. The light from the candles moved a little. And there was my ghost, with his strange gestures. He tried for a minute or two, then he sat on the little chair by the bed. "I can't do it!" he said. "I shall never get back!" And then he started to cry.

gesture /ˈdʒestʃə/ (n/v) You move your arms, hands or head when you make a *gesture*.

'I put my hand on his back. I wanted to be kind to him. But my hand went through him and I pulled it away.

'"Now," I said to him, "try again. I'll try too. We'll do it at the same time."'

'What do you mean?' said Evans. '*You* tried the gestures?'

'Yes. I wanted to help him.'

'This is very interesting,' said Sanderson. 'He showed you the gestures? The way back to the other world?'

'Yes.'

'But he went, and you didn't.'

For a short time nobody spoke. It was very quiet in the room.

'And then he did it? He went?' I asked.

'Yes, he did it,' Clayton said. 'He tried and tried. I tried with him. We went back to the start and tried again. I made the gestures slowly and he watched carefully. Then he said, "Don't watch me. I'll do it better that way." So I turned my back to him. I looked at the window and he stood behind me. He made the gestures. I could see him in the window. For the last gesture he put his arms out like this …'

Clayton stood and showed us the last gesture.

'And then he went! He wasn't there! I turned back to the room, but my ghost wasn't there. I was the only person in the bedroom. And that's the end of his story.'

'So then you went to bed?' asked Evans.

'Yes, I did.'

'Tell us more about these gestures,' said Sanderson.

'I think I can do them all now,' Clayton said.

'They won't work,' said Evans. 'Nothing will happen.'

'Perhaps they *will* work,' I said. 'And then …'

'I don't think this is a good idea,' said Wish. He looked afraid.

'He won't get the gestures right,' said Sanderson. 'So it will be all right.'

Clayton stood in front of the fire.

'I've got a problem with one gesture,' he said. 'I can't get it quite right. Look.'

He showed us the gesture. At the end, it didn't look right. We could see that.

'Try it this way …' said Sanderson, and he moved his hands in a different way. Clayton tried again. It looked better.

'Now I can do everything,' said Clayton. 'Watch. This is the start …'

'Stop!' said Wish. 'Don't do this. I think it's dangerous.'

'Why?' asked Evans. 'Nothing

will happen. Clayton won't go into the world of ghosts. He's a person. He's a big, strong man – not a thin little ghost. Look at him!'

'Wish is afraid,' I said.

Wish stood up.

'Clayton,' he said, 'You're stupid. This is a stupid game. Stop it now.' But Clayton smiled at him. He didn't want to stop.

'Perhaps Wish is right, and you are all wrong,' he said. 'Perhaps I will go. Let's try. Let's see.'

He started doing the gestures. We all watched him. Nobody said a word. He came to the last gesture. Nobody moved.

He stood for a minute with his arms open. The light from the candles shone on his face. We all watched and waited. Nothing happened.

And then Clayton's face changed. There was a sudden change in his eyes. His smile went. He stood there, and then, very slowly, he started to fall.

We all moved quickly to him. Evans was there first, and Clayton fell into his arms.

For a short time, nobody spoke. Clayton was on the floor. Sanderson felt inside his shirt, but there was no life.

We could do nothing for him.

'And now Clayton is in the ghost world! I was afraid of this,' Wish cried.

'Why did this happen?' we asked. There was no answer. Perhaps it was because of the gestures, and the ghost. But we will all have to die. Perhaps this was Clayton's time and the gestures were not important. I don't know.

But I do know this. Clayton finished the gestures, and in the very next minute he fell down – dead!

1 **Work with another student. Remember the story of 'The Young Ghost' and have this conversation.**

Student A   You are Clayton's sister. You want to know more about your brother's last night. You know nothing about the ghost. What do you want to ask his friend Wish? Think about your questions and make notes. Then ask them.

Student B   You are Wish. You feel very sorry for Miss Clayton. What are you going to tell her? Think about your answers. Then answer her questions. Remember: you wanted Clayton to stop!

2 **Work with other students. Remember the story of 'The Door in the Wall'.**

Wallace saw many things in the garden, but they are not in this picture. What is not there? Discuss this and write them below.

1 ....   5 ....

2 ....   6 ....

3 ....   7 ....

4 ....   8 ....

1 After the story of 'The Country of the Blind', Nunez arrives home in Bogotá and tells other climbers about the valley. You and some friends plan a visit there. What will you take with you for the journey? What will you take for the villagers?

For the journey:

1 ....

2 ....

3 ....

4 ....

5 ....

6 ....

7 ....

8 ....

For the villagers:

9 ....

10 ....

11 ....

12 ....

13 ....

14 ....

Talk to other students about your ideas. What did you forget? Write them above.

1 **Work with two or three other students.**

a Read this story from a British magazine in 1950.

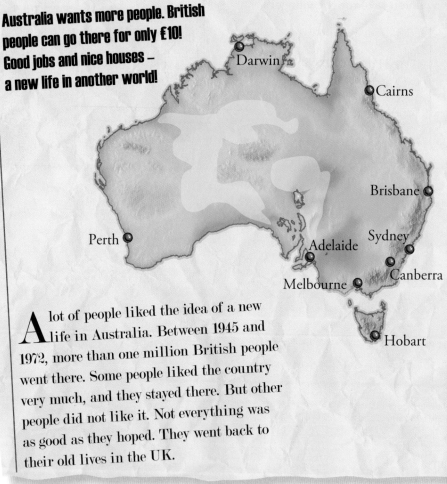

Australia wants more people. British people can go there for only £10! Good jobs and nice houses – a new life in another world!

Darwin

Cairns

Brisbane

Perth

Adelaide

Sydney

Melbourne

Canberra

Hobart

A lot of people liked the idea of a new life in Australia. Between 1945 and 1972, more than one million British people went there. Some people liked the country very much, and they stayed there. But other people did not like it. Not everything was as good as they hoped. They went back to their old lives in the UK.

b Discuss these questions and write notes.

Why did people stay in Australia?   Why did people leave again?

....

....

....

2 Look at these pictures. These people also went a long way for a better life. They arrived first, and a lot of other people followed them.

Discuss the questions below. Find out more from the Internet.

'The New World' of America, 1620, 300 people

London, 1948, 100 men

a Who were these people?

b Where did they come from?

c What problems do you think they had in their new lives?

d Why do you think they made the long journeys?

Write a postcard home from one of the people in the pictures above.

4 You work for a TV company and you have a new idea for 'The Village'. Your company is going a build a small village in the north of Scotland, a very long way from the nearest town. There will be six houses and some animals. Then you will send 30 people there for six months and TV cameras will film their new lives. First, you have to find your 30 people. Write this advertisement for a magazine.

Do you want to be on television?
We are looking for 30 people!

They will have to ....
....

Are you:
- .... ?
- .... ?
- .... ?

Is your life now:
- .... ?
- .... ?

Would you like:
- .... ?
- .... ?

Can you:
- .... ?
- .... ?

Am I looking for you?

Write to me: ....

at: Northern TV Studios, Television House, Station Street, Manchester